Training the Youth Athlete

DAN JOHN

Contents

*For my mother, Aileen Barbara McCloskey John.
She understood "all of this." She never concerned
herself with wins or losses, but literally with how
we played the game.*

*And to my friends that we lost that terrible
August day.*

Introduction

I've been a paid strength coach since 1979. Training programs, fitness celebrities, fads, and fashions have come and gone, but some things really haven't changed at all: the human body and progressive resistance exercise.

Tom Delorme coined the idea of progressive resistance exercise (PRE), assisting the injured after World War II. PRE has spun off in countless directions, but the focus on proper technique, appropriate load, reps, and sets still remains the essential core and truth of training. The basics worked with G.I. Joe and continue to work today.

We seem to be past the period when lifting was somehow **"suspect,"** making one musclebound and morally bankrupt. It's not unusual today to visit senior centers and witness trainees lifting iron and pushing plates. We are also seeing young athletes exposed to the basics and fundamentals of the weight room.

It wasn't long ago that weights, and I believe it was said about coffee also, would **"stunt one's growth."** Like many tall tales, this myth disappeared years ago. However, it is not unusual today to see young athletes pushed into aggressive training programs with far too much load, far too early.

Recently, I have been asked to speak on youth weightlifting both here in the United States and in Europe. As I began assembling my materials, I realized it might be wise to share this with all of you.

Sports, games, and training for them teach lessons that continue to bless the child throughout their life. Besides learning the discipline of showing up, showing up prepared, and on time, many of us learned to trust one another and to work with others, of all backgrounds, for a greater goal. That is a life lesson worth learning.

The first chapter provides a short overview of coaching. The next three chapters focus on issues that concern me about modern youth training, including early specialization, attempts to overload movement patterns, and, of course, issues surrounding puberty.

From there, I will introduce my vision for strength and athletic conditioning for younger athletes. We will focus on developing mastery in age-appropriate ways. There will also be chapters to help coaches *"coach"* parents to support their children. Nutrition and supplements will be discussed, as these are increasingly important issues each year.

The next chapters will introduce the ideas of ***"level changes"*** in training. There is more to strength training than sitting on a seat pushing a handle. Tumbling, groundwork, and the joy of movement should be standards in every youth program.

The focus of this work is to prepare the young athlete for life and all its demands. We will not focus on building a bigger arm or a tighter tummy, although this can certainly be a by-product. The final line is this:

> ***"Our job is to raise capable adults."***

As I sneak into the seventh decade of my life, I can't imagine a higher calling.

Coaching: The Big Picture

If you coach long enough, you begin to notice something: the loudest voices in youth sports are rarely the ones doing the daily work.

I love sports. I love practices, growth, progress, and the quiet satisfaction of improvement. What I don't love is the sideline expert who has never tried to reteach footwork to a distracted twelve-year-old or calm a teenager who just cost the team a game. That perspective matters.

Before we dive into drills, systems, and practice plans, it helps to step back and look at the big picture of youth coaching.

Years ago, I explained coaching levels using comedy. I described the spectrum of being funny, from telling a joke with friends, to performing a five-minute stand-up set, to becoming a true entertainer. Think of someone like Gene Kelly, or in a more recent era, performers such as Hannah Waddingham or Hugh Jackman. Every generation has people who can dance, sing, make you laugh, and move you emotionally. The analogy still fits coaching.

Level One is the Drill Caller. This coach runs a station. Whistle. Drill. Correction. Move on. There is nothing wrong with this; it is necessary. But it is surface-level. It focuses on activity rather than development.

Level Two is the Practice Leader. This coach reads the group, adjusts when energy drops, changes tone when frustration rises, and balances correction with encouragement. This level requires awareness and flexibility. It is more than running drills; it is managing people.

Level Three is the Developer of People. This is master-level youth coaching. This coach teaches skills, but also builds confidence, resilience, and character. They understand that growth is uneven. They know when to push and when to protect. They see beyond this weekend's scoreboard.

Most spectators evaluate Level One. Great youth coaches live at Level Three. Our job is not to win the weekend; our job is to move young people forward.

The word **coach** originally referred to a carriage, a vehicle that carried someone from one place to another. That is still the job. We take a young athlete from shy to confident, from clumsy to coordinated, from self-doubt to self-belief, and from emotional reaction to emotional control. Much of coaching is simply keeping them in the vehicle long enough to reach their destination.

Do not let them walk out because they missed a shot. Do not let them quit because someone else made the A team. Do not let them bail because it got hard. Youth coaching sometimes feels like the warning at an amusement park: keep your hands, arms, feet, and legs inside the ride at all times. Keep them inside the process. That is development.

One of the most useful coaching lessons I encountered came from the book **Think Like a Freak** by Steven Levitt and Stephen Dubner. It is technically about economics, but it is really about thinking clearly. Two ideas from that book apply directly to youth coaching.

The first is that knowing what to measure simplifies life. In youth sports, we measure the wrong things far too often: scoreboards, playing time, and tournament trophies. Those are outcomes. Better metrics look different. Did the athlete improve a skill? Did they give consistent effort? Did they respond better to correction this month than last month? Did they support a teammate? Did they come back after failure? If a young athlete leaves your program more confident, more capable, and more resilient than when they entered, you were right, even if the record book disagrees. Clarity comes from choosing the right scoreboard.

The second idea is just as simple: do not fear the obvious. If you want kids to improve, they need repetition, feedback, sleep, food, encouragement, and time. There are no secrets. Parents sometimes lean forward as if you are about to reveal a hidden formula. The formula is consistency. Tired athletes need rest. Uncoordinated athletes need basic movement practice. Insecure athletes need small, repeated wins. Do not overcomplicate what does not need to be complicated.

There is a well-known story about the golfer Gary Player. After a rough round, a fan shouted, *"I'd trade my best day for your worst day."* Player reportedly replied, *"No, you wouldn't. You don't want the work. You just want the result."* I once asked him about this at the Delta Sky Club in Atlanta when we were both getting chicken noodle soup, and he smiled and said the story was *"true enough."*

That sentiment applies directly to youth sports. Many people want confident kids, but few want the slow, repetitive, sometimes boring process that builds confidence. Many want mentally tough athletes, but few are willing to let them struggle long enough to develop toughness. As coaches, we must stay committed to the process even when others crave shortcuts.

Part of that commitment involves language. Every word we use carries baggage. For some young athletes, conditioning means punishment. Defense means embarrassment. Practice means boring. Mistake means shame. You say, *"We're going to work on fundamentals,"* and they hear, *"This is going to hurt."*

Coaching, at its best, is translation. A mistake becomes information. Conditioning becomes building an engine. Practice becomes where confidence is earned. If you do not redefine these words, someone else will, and that definition rarely supports development.

If there is a secret to youth coaching, it is this: be outstanding in your field, literally. You have to be out there in the early mornings, after school, on cold evenings and hot afternoons, repetition after repetition. You cannot rush coordination, emotional maturity, confidence, character, or childhood itself.

The best youth coaches I know are patient. They test ideas, discard trends, refine systems, and relearn lessons over years rather than months. Coaching youth is both science and art. You need structure and progressions. You should study movement and development. But you also need to feel. You need to sense when a group is overwhelmed, recognize when a child is shutting down, and know when to push and when to protect.

It is like cooking. You may have a recipe, but the ingredients change daily: different personalities, maturity levels, home environments, and emotional states. Rigid plans rarely survive contact with a group of young athletes at the end of a long school day.

Good coaching is more than instruction. It is translation between potential and performance, between who a child is today and who they might become tomorrow. You can design the perfect session on paper, but if half your team walks in discouraged or exhausted, the art of coaching begins.

The foundation of youth development is simple: understand the long-term goal, assess continuously, and adjust compassionately. The goal is growth over time. The assessment is daily. The art is knowing what today requires.

Good coaching is more than instruction. It is translation between potential and performance, between where a child stands today and who they might become tomorrow. Percy Cerutty, the great Australian track and field coach, once warned:

> *"The teachings of the coach must always be suspect when he attempts to develop techniques based upon theories worked out intellectually. Unless he gets the idea from personal experience and feelings first, he is most likely to be wrong in principle."*

You can design the perfect session on paper, but if half your team walks in discouraged, distracted, or exhausted, the art of coaching begins. The foundation of youth development is straightforward: understand the long-term goal, assess continuously, and adjust compassionately. The goal is not immediate perfection. It is growth over time. Assessment happens daily, and the art lies in recognizing what is required today.

That is the big picture of youth coaching. Move them forward, keep them in the vehicle, and stay in the field long enough for growth to happen.

Keep them in the coach, coach!

Youth Athletes and Year-Round Specialization

I have never been a big fan of young athletes training year-round in one sport. I know there are exceptions. There are always exceptions. But when I look back over decades of coaching, the athletes who lasted the longest and performed the best were rarely the ones who specialized early.

They were the kids who played everything.

They played football in the fall, basketball in the winter, and ran track in the spring. In the summer, they swam, rode bikes, or just ran around with their friends. They climbed trees, jumped fences, and spent long days outside. They were not following a twelve-month training plan. They were growing up.

And that matters.

Different sports develop different qualities. Football teaches contact, acceleration, and courage. Basketball teaches footwork, timing, and awareness. Track and field builds speed, power, and discipline. Baseball and softball teach patience, timing, and rotational power. Wrestling builds toughness and body awareness.

Each sport fills in gaps left by the others.

When a young athlete specializes too early, those gaps never get filled. The body develops in a narrow pattern. The same movements, the same stresses, and the same joints get hammered over and over again.

Eventually, something gives.

Sometimes it is an overuse injury. Sometimes it is burnout. Sometimes the athlete simply loses the joy of the sport. When the game becomes a year-round obligation at twelve or thirteen years old, the spark can disappear.

I have seen it too many times. The best twelve-year-old in the state never plays in college. The kid who was *"all in"* on one sport at ten years old is done with that sport at sixteen.

Meanwhile, the multi-sport athlete keeps improving. They may not look as polished at fourteen, but at eighteen they are strong, coordinated, and resilient. At twenty-two, they are still playing, still training, and still enjoying the process.

Part of this comes down to simple wear and tear. The human body was not designed to throw year-round, or to swing a bat year-round, or to kick a soccer ball year-round. Repetition without variation leads to breakdown.

But there is also a neurological and developmental side to this.

Young athletes need a wide base of movement. They need to run, jump, throw, catch, tumble, crawl, climb, and balance. Each sport gives them a different set of problems to solve. Each sport teaches them new patterns and new skills.

This variety builds a more complete athlete.

It also builds a more complete person.

Different teams have different cultures. Different coaches have different expectations. Different sports create different friendships. All of this helps the young athlete grow socially and emotionally.

There is also the simple reality of puberty. Bodies change at different rates. The early maturing athlete often dominates youth sports. They are bigger, stronger, and faster than their peers.

But puberty is not a straight line.

The late developer often catches up. The athlete who struggled at thirteen may shine at seventeen. But if that athlete specialized early, got injured, or burned out, they may never reach that stage.

Multi-sport participation keeps doors open.

It allows the athlete to grow, adapt, and discover where they truly belong. It also gives their body a break. When one sport ends, another begins, often with different demands and different movement patterns.

That seasonal change is built in recovery.

I am not against commitment. I am not against hard work. And I understand that certain sports, like gymnastics or figure skating, may require earlier specialization. But those are the exceptions, not the rule.

For most youth athletes, the goal should be simple: play a lot of sports, move in a lot of ways, and keep the joy in the process.

In the long run, the athlete who builds a broad base usually wins.

Summary: The Case Against Year-Round Specialization

- Most successful long-term athletes played multiple sports as youths.

- Different sports develop different physical and mental qualities.

- Year-round repetition in one sport increases injury risk.

- Early specialization often leads to burnout.

- Puberty changes the playing field, and early stars do not always stay ahead.

- Multi-sport participation builds a broader athletic and social foundation.

- Seasonal sport changes provide natural recovery.

Conclusion: What Should Youth Athletes Do?

For most young athletes, the best plan is simple:

1. Play different sports throughout the year.

2. Build general strength, coordination, and movement skills.

3. Avoid year-round repetition of the same patterns.

4. Keep training fun and varied.

5. Focus on long term development, not short-term trophies.

In other words: Play more. Specialize later. Stay healthy. And keep the joy in sport.

Train the Athlete, Not the Exercise

I've never been a big believer in sport specific strength exercises. That usually surprises people, because I spent most of my life around high-level sport. I threw the discus. I coached throwers, football players, and a lot of other athletes. So, people assume I must have a secret list of magical exercises that transfer directly to the field.

I don't.

What I do believe in is preparing the athlete. The sport takes care of the sport.

If you are a basketball player, the most specific thing you can do is play basketball. If you are a thrower, the most specific thing you can do is throw. If you are a football player, the most specific thing you can do is play football. Once you start trying to imitate the sport in the weight room, things tend to get silly in a hurry.

You see it all the time. Someone straps bands around their waist, stands on a wobble board, holds a cable, and performs something that vaguely looks like a golf swing or a tennis stroke. The problem is simple. It looks like the sport, but it is not the sport. The speeds are wrong. The forces are wrong. The timing is wrong. And most of the time, the technique is wrong too.

So, what have we really trained?

Usually, we have just practiced a bad version of the sport with light resistance and poor mechanics.

The weight room is for general qualities: strength, power, mobility, work capacity, and armor. The field, court, or ring is for skill.

I learned this lesson early. When I was throwing, I spent a lot of time doing things that had nothing to do with the discus. I squatted. I cleaned. I pressed. I did pull ups and carries. None of those movements looked like a discus throw. But when I stepped into the ring, I was stronger, more stable, and more explosive.

That was the transfer.

The body does not always need a perfect imitation of the sport. It needs bigger engines, stronger frames, and better movement. If the athlete is stronger in the hinge, more stable in the squat, more powerful in the Olympic lifts, and more resilient from loaded carries, good things tend to happen in competition.

The mistake comes when we confuse the weight room with the practice field. The weight room is a support system. It fills in the gaps. It builds the qualities that the sport itself does not fully develop.

Most sports already provide plenty of skill work, reaction, and conditioning. What they often lack is simple, progressive strength training. Instead of fixing that, coaches sometimes try to turn the weight room into a strange, low-quality version of the sport.

It is almost always better to separate the two. Practice the sport with full intent and full speed. Then go to the weight room and train the fundamental human movements: push, pull, hinge, squat, carry, and sometimes a bit of rotation and anti-rotation.

If you get those right, most of the so-called sport specific issues solve themselves.

There is also a safety issue. When you try to mimic sport movements under load, you often place the athlete in compromised positions. The barbell or cable does not understand the flow of the game. It just adds force. And force in the wrong position is how people get hurt.

Simple lifts done well are safer. They are easier to teach, easier to load, and easier to progress. They also allow the athlete to come back the next day and actually practice the sport.

I remind coaches of a simple idea: do not steal from the sport. If your weight room leaves the athlete too tired, too sore, or too beat up to practice well, you have failed. The sport is the main course. The weight room is the side dish.

In my experience, the best athletes I ever coached did very basic training. They lifted, they carried, they jumped, and they threw. Nothing looked fancy. But they were strong, fast, and durable. And that is what shows up on the scoreboard.

So instead of chasing sport specific exercises, focus on athlete specific needs. Where are the gaps? What qualities are missing? What can we build in the weight room that the sport itself does not provide?

Answer those questions, and the program usually writes itself.

In the end, the goal is simple. Train the athlete. Practice the sport. Keep those two ideas clear, and most of the confusion disappears.

Five Problems with Sport Specific Training

1. **It usually becomes a bad imitation of the sport.**
   The speeds, forces, and timing are never the same.

2. **It confuses practice with training.**
   The field is for skill. The weight room is for physical qualities.

3. **It steals time and energy from real practice.**
   If the athlete cannot perform well in the sport, the program is wrong.

4. **It increases injury risk.**
   Adding load to awkward, sport like positions often creates problems.

5. **It ignores the real gaps.**
   Most athletes do not need a cable golf swing. They need stronger hips, better posture, and more resilience.

Puberty and the Athlete

Simply, puberty is the process when a child becomes an adult.

And there is nothing simple about that.

Working with youth athletes presents dozens, perhaps hundreds, even thousands of challenges. No matter where we begin studying those challenges, puberty, like a Hydra, seems to multiply problems faster than we can address them.

For the coach, society and technology change constantly. My parents worried when we went into another room to use the landline telephone. Another generation may have feared bears or lions when a child wandered out of sight. As I write this, many parents fear online predators of a very different kind. Fashions change. Fads come and go. The language, the phrases, and the trends shift so quickly that even the most interested adults struggle to keep up.

I walked away from pop music in the early 1970s, popular movies a decade later, and *"must see"* television not long after that. I have never really understood the role of social media influencers. But my athletes take these things very seriously.

At the same time, their bodies are changing radically. Drastically. I entered my freshman year of high school weighing 118 pounds. When I reported for the spring of my freshman year of college, I weighed 218 pounds. For my non-American friends, that is a jump from about 53 kilograms to roughly 100 kilograms in four years. I nearly doubled in size.

The teen years, and we could certainly move the start of puberty earlier for many female athletes and extend it into the early twenties for some males, are a journey for all of us. The social struggles are well captured in the John Hughes films, but there are also the ravages of acne, awkwardness in every form, and a thousand other issues that affect the youth athlete.

I often summarize the challenges of being a teen athlete with this simple example: in my high school math class, I sat next to a girl who was married. I had never even been on a date. We were the same age.

Same age, yet massive life differences.

I keep a few ideas in mind when I work with youth athletes.

It took me a few years to recognize the following point. A fellow coach, our girls' soccer coach, once said, ***"We might struggle this year, but we have a crop of freshman girls (about fourteen years old) who are just going to dominate."*** A few years later, he said the exact same thing again. It took me a while to process this, until my own daughters went to high school.

Gymnastics and a few other sports often favor the pre-adolescent female athlete. When certain traits of puberty begin, performance can change quickly. One example is the increase in the Q angle, which can affect both performance and injury risk. (I will share more on the Q angle later.)

At the same time, while the female athlete's body is changing, there are, at least among American athletes, social pressures that can wreak havoc on the aspiring athlete. Getting a date to Homecoming or Prom may seem unimportant to many of us, but it can be overwhelming to someone in high school. Body image issues are real. Social pressures are real.

High school can be a difficult time for the female athlete.

They are not alone.

The next point relates to winning the race to manhood on the boys' athletic field. My good friend Steve was a Hall of Fame baseball coach here in Utah. We both volunteered at a number of the same events, and I learned so much from him about throwing.

I also learned an important truth from him about recruiting boy athletes. He told me the story of a young boy who struck fear into the hearts of his opponents. In the eighth grade, this young man already had a bit of a mustache and beard and towered over his teammates. He threw in the high seventies and dominated as a pitcher.

The story continued. Steve noted, ***"He was a man."*** The boy was blessed with early puberty and dominated opponents who were probably still spending their nights putting together Legos and battling He-Man with Skeletor. Within a year or two, though, he was still the same height, weight, and power, while his teammates grew taller, bigger, and stronger in the weight room and on the athletic field. Our friend's fastball never improved, and he never developed the work ethic to stay ahead of his peers.

Steve went on to explain something that is hard to grasp: as coaches, we can fall in love with the early developer. We invent a future of continued growth, more improvement, and championship banners.

Contrast that with another boy I coached. Let's call him Dave. We were sitting in a coaches' meeting when a colleague said, ***"I can't believe that in two years we're going to have to count on some kid like Dave to bail us out."***

Time passed. Dave trained hard and, with the help of puberty, grew into a physical specimen.

Two years and a bit later, the same coach said, ***"How are we ever going to replace Dave?"***

If I were Aesop, I would have a moral to these stories. I'm not Aesop, but I do have a lesson.

Conclusion

Puberty is not a straight line, and athletic development is not a prediction contest. The early developer is not guaranteed greatness, and the late bloomer is not destined to be a role player. Bodies change. Priorities shift. Confidence rises and falls. Social pressures come and go.

Our job as coaches is not to guess who will win the race through puberty. Our job is to build habits, skills, and character that last beyond it.

Train them all. Teach them all. Care for them all.

Because the fourteen-year-old star might struggle at sixteen, and the awkward kid in the corner might be the one carrying your program at eighteen.

What Is the Q Angle?

The **Q angle**, or quadriceps angle, is a measurement used to describe the alignment of the hip, knee, and lower leg.

The simple explanation

The Q angle is the angle formed by two lines:

1. A line from the front of the hip (the anterior superior iliac spine).

2. A line from the kneecap down to the tibial tuberosity (just below the knee).

This angle shows how the quadriceps muscle pulls on the kneecap.

Why it matters

- A **larger Q angle** means the thigh bone angles more inward toward the knee.

- This changes how forces travel through the knee joint.

- It can increase stress on the kneecap and surrounding structures.

Differences between males and females

During puberty:

- The **female pelvis widens** to prepare for childbirth.

- This naturally **increases the Q angle**.

- As a result, many girls experience:

- Changes in running and jumping mechanics.

- A temporary drop in coordination or performance.

- A higher risk of certain knee injuries, especially ACL injuries.

Typical averages:

- Males: about **10 to 14 degrees**

- Females: about **15 to 20 degrees**

These are general ranges, not strict rules.

Coaching implications

For the coach, the increase in Q angle means:

- Movement patterns may change during puberty.

- Some athletes who were dominant at 12 or 13 may struggle at 15 or 16.

- Strength and movement training becomes more important.

Key training focuses:

- Glute strength

- Hip stability

- Landing mechanics

- Single leg balance and control

In simple terms, puberty changes the structure of the athlete. When the structure changes, the movement changes. And when movement changes, performance and injury risk both change.

Training the Athlete

When I look back over my career, one idea keeps showing up again and again:

Train the athlete. Do not just train the exercise.

It is easy to get distracted by exercises. New movements appear every year. New machines. New systems. New certifications. The fitness industry loves novelty.

But the human body has not changed.

We still hinge, squat, push, pull, carry, crawl, climb, and rotate. Those are the movements that matter. Those are the movements that show up in sport, in work, and in life.

The real question for a coach is simple: what does this athlete need?

That is where the idea of standards and gaps comes in. First, we establish reasonable standards. Can the athlete hinge? Can they squat? Can they carry their bodyweight? Can they do a pull up? Can they move with balance and control?

Then we look at the gap between where they are and where they should be.

That gap tells us what to train.

Notice what is missing from that process. We did not start with a list of exercises. We started with the athlete.

Too many programs are built the other way around. The coach has a favorite lift, a favorite system, or a favorite piece of equipment. Then every athlete, no matter the sport or the need, is forced into that system.

That is backwards.

The athlete comes first. The program serves the athlete. The exercise is just a tool.

Sometimes the right tool is a barbell. Sometimes it is a kettlebell. Sometimes it is a sled. Sometimes it is a simple walk around the field.

If the athlete needs more posterior chain strength, we hinge. If they lack stability, we carry. If they lack coordination, we tumble or crawl. If they lack work capacity, we walk.

Over time, the athlete becomes stronger, more resilient, and more capable. That is the goal.

Exercises come and go. Trends change. But the athlete remains. So keep the focus where it belongs:

Train the athlete.
Let the sport handle the sport.
And let the exercises stay in their proper place: as tools, not the goal.

Red Flags and Green Flags in Youth Training

How to Know Where Your Athlete Should Be

Youth training doesn't have to be complicated.

But it does require discernment. There are good coaches doing excellent work with young athletes. There are also environments that look impressive on the surface but quietly undermine long-term development.

Instead of arguing theory, let's make this simple.

Here's what to watch for.

Red Flags

If You See This, Ask Questions — Or Walk Away

1. Adult Programs Shrunk Down for Kids

If the program looks like it was copied from a college football strength manual and handed to a 12-year-old, pause.

Kids are not small adults.

They don't need max-effort days every week.
They don't need complex periodization charts.
They don't need brutal finishers.

They need skill, repetition, coordination, and gradual exposure to load.

Development first. Always.

2. Conditioning Used as Punishment

If missed shots equal sprints...
If mistakes equal push-ups...
If losing equals laps...

That's not character development.

That's laziness.

Conditioning should build capacity, not shame. When effort becomes punishment, kids learn to avoid effort instead of embrace it.

Hard work is a gift. Don't weaponize it.

3. Heavy Loading Before Technical Mastery

If a young athlete cannot:

- Hinge well

- Squat with control

- Brace properly

- Land softly

They are not ready to chase numbers under a barbell.

Load magnifies flaws.

Teach movement. Then add load. There is no scholarship for *"earliest max deadlift."*

4. Early Specialization

If a 10-year-old is told to focus on one sport year-round, be cautious.

Before puberty, variety builds:

- Coordination

- Elasticity

- Awareness

- Adaptability

A broad base protects the athlete later.

Narrow too early, and the system cracks under pressure.

5. Supplements Pushed on Middle Schoolers

If 11-year-olds are being sold stacks of powders...

If 13-year-olds are encouraged to take pre-workouts...

If fat burners are part of the conversation...

Leave.

Young athletes need food, sleep, water, and coaching.

Not stimulants.

6. Public Shaming Disguised as Toughness

Humiliation is not leadership.

Embarrassment does not build resilience.

Real toughness is built through:

- Consistency
- Gradual challenge
- Trust

Fear shrinks performance. Trust expands it.

7. Performance Over Health

If athletes are:

- Training through pain regularly
- Playing year-round without breaks
- Rewarded for hiding injuries

That's not grit.

That's negligence.

The goal of youth training is a 20-year runway, not a two-year high-light reel.

Green Flags

Signs You're in the Right Place

Now let's flip the lens.

If you see these things, exhale. You're probably in good hands.

1. Movement Before Load

You see kids learning to:

- Squat well
- Hinge properly
- Land softly
- Sprint with rhythm

Weights are light. Coaching is patient. Corrections are calm.

They're building foundations.

2. The Coach Is Watching

The coach isn't just blowing a whistle.

They're observing.

They kneel down.
They adjust hand position.
They change drills when something isn't working.
They shorten sessions when attention fades.

Engagement over ego.

3. Kids Look Challenged — But Safe

There's effort.

There's sweat.

There's frustration.

But there's no fear.

No flinching.
No bracing for embarrassment.
No public humiliation.

They are working — and they know they are supported.

4. Variety Is Built In

You see:

- Games

- Carries

- Crawling

- Jumping

- Throwing

- Sprinting

- Basic strength

It looks like preparation for a lifetime of movement — not a tryout for a professional combine.

5. Progress Is Measured in Skill and Confidence

The coach celebrates:

- Cleaner reps

- Better posture

- Composure after mistakes

- Effort

- Leadership

It's not just about the number on the bar.

It's about growth.

6. Parents Are Educated, Not Sold To

You hear conversations about:

- Sleep
- Nutrition
- Patience
- Long-term development

You don't hear scholarship promises.

You don't see pressure tactics.

There's transparency.

7. Rest Is Respected

There are off-seasons.

There are breaks.

There are lighter weeks.

No one panics when an athlete plays another sport or takes time off.

The program understands that growth happens during recovery.

8. The Best Athlete Still Trains the Basics

Watch the most talented kid in the room.

If they're still practicing fundamentals, you're in the right place.

If stars skip the base work, development eventually collapses.

9. The Environment Feels Calm

Not frantic.

Not chaotic.

Not urgent.

There's rhythm.

The coach isn't trying to prove something.

They're building something.

The 20-Year Vision

Here is the question that clarifies everything:

"What will this athlete look like at 30?"

Not at 14.
Not at 16.
Not even at 18.

At 30.

Will they:

- Still love to train?

- Still move well?

- Still be injury-free?

- Still see strength as part of their identity?

- Still enjoy sport and competition?

Or will they be burned out, broken down, and done? Youth training should expand possibility, not compress it. If we do this right, the athlete leaves high school stronger than when they started, but more importantly, healthier, more confident, and more capable.

The goal is not early domination. The goal is durable development. Build the base. Protect the runway. Play the long game.

If the environment supports that vision, stay.

If it doesn't, you already know what to do.

Strength Training and the Youth Athlete

For all my concerns about early specialization, year-round competition, and sport specific nonsense in the weight room, I do believe that strength training makes a real difference in youth sports.

A big difference.

But, as always, the key is how it is done and why it is done.

I have never believed that young athletes need complicated programs. They do not need periodized spreadsheets, advanced plyometrics, or the latest gadget from a fitness expo. What they need is simple, sensible strength training built around fundamental human movements.

When a young athlete learns to hinge, squat, push, pull, carry, crawl, and tumble, good things happen. They move better. They feel more confident. They become more resilient. And those qualities show up in every sport.

Strength is a universal quality. It transfers.

A stronger athlete can usually run faster, jump higher, and hold better positions on the field or court. A stronger athlete also tends to get hurt less. When the joints are supported by stronger muscles and better movement patterns, the body can tolerate more stress.

That is one of the quiet benefits of strength training. It does not just make you better. It often keeps you in the game long enough to become better.

I have seen this over and over again. The athletes who learn how to lift, carry, and control their bodies tend to last. They may not always be the most skilled at fourteen, but at eighteen they are often the ones still competing, still improving, and still enjoying the process.

Strength training also teaches important life lessons.

It teaches patience. Strength takes time. It teaches consistency. You have to show up again and again. It teaches humility. The bar does not care about your excuses. And it teaches confidence. There is something powerful about picking up a heavy object and realizing that you can do hard things.

These lessons carry over into school, work, and life.

But we have to be careful with young athletes. The goal is not to turn a twelve-year-old into a powerlifter. The goal is not to chase one rep maxes or post videos of record lifts on social media.

The goal is preparation.

For young athletes, the weight room should be a place to learn movement, build general strength, and develop good habits. Most of the time, bodyweight movements, light implements, and simple barbell lifts are more than enough.

Goblet squats. Push ups. Pull ups. Farmer walks. Hip hinges. Medicine ball throws. Simple presses. Maybe some basic Olympic lift variations when the athlete is ready.

Nothing fancy. Nothing extreme. Just good, solid training done consistently.

Another benefit of strength training is that it helps level the playing field during puberty. Young athletes develop at different rates. The early maturer often dominates because they are bigger and stronger.

But strength training gives the late maturer a tool. They may not be the biggest athlete, but they can become stronger, more stable, and more coordinated. Over time, that makes a difference.

Strength training also helps athletes handle the demands of multiple sports. If the athlete has a solid base of strength, they can move from football to basketball to track without breaking down. Their body is prepared for the variety.

That is another reason I prefer general strength training over sport specific exercises. General strength supports everything. It builds the foundation.

The sport sits on top of that foundation.

If the foundation is weak, the structure eventually cracks. If the foundation is strong, the athlete can adapt to almost any demand.

So yes, I believe in strength training for youth athletes. I just believe in the right kind of strength training.

Keep it simple.
Keep it safe.
Keep it focused on the fundamentals.
And remember the real goal: build the athlete, not the numbers on the bar.

Over time, that approach almost always wins.

Youth Movement Matrix

The Youth Version of the Movement Matrix

When we train young athletes, we are not preparing them for the next game. We are preparing them for the next decade. Maybe even the next half century. That changes everything.

Adults train to improve performance. Kids train to build the person who will someday perform.

The Movement Matrix gives us a simple way to think about this. Every human being needs to push, pull, hinge, squat, carry, and move through space. These are not sport skills. These are human skills. Sport is just a more complicated expression of them.

With youth athletes, the Matrix doesn't change. The movements stay the same. What changes is the expression.

Movement	Planks as a Program	Strength Training (Less then 10 reps) / Hypertrophy (15-25 reps)	Anti-Rotation Work	Traids	Olympic Lifts
Push	**PUPPs** Plank	(Bench) Press Push-up	1 Arm Bench Press 1 Arm Overhead Press	Push press / jerk	Squat Snatch
Pull	**TRX Rows** Bat Wing Ts and Ys	Pull-up Row	1 arm TRX Row	Swing	
Hinge	**Gluteal Bridge** with AB Hold	Hip Thrust Rack DLs Goat Bag Swing	**Hill Sprints / Stadium Steps** Skipping / Bounding / High Knee Work	Liftsprints, Liftsleds	Clean & Jerk
Squat	**Goblet Squats** 6 point Rocks	Dbl KB Front Squat The Whole Squat Family	**Bear Hug Carries** Bear Crawls Bear Hug Carries with Monster Walk		
Loaded Carry	**Farmer's Walk** Horn Walk	Prowler Car push	1 arm carries: **Suitcase Carry** Walter Walk Rack Walk		

Note: a larger version of the Matrix can be found in Appendix Three

A squat for an adult might be a heavy back squat. A squat for a ten-year-old might be a goblet squat with a light kettlebell or simply sitting down and standing up from a box. Same pattern. Different load. Different expectations.

A hinge for an adult might be a heavy deadlift. For a young athlete, it might be a glute bridge, a light kettlebell deadlift, or a medicine ball throw. The goal is not numbers. The goal is understanding the movement.

The biggest mistake in youth training is skipping the foundation. Coaches rush to barbells, complex programs, and sport-specific drills before the athlete can even perform a clean push-up or a solid goblet squat. That is a gap, and gaps always come back to haunt you.

In the youth version of the Matrix, we start with play and body-weight. Crawling, skipping, tumbling, hanging, and carrying objects are not just warm-ups. They are the program. These movements build coordination, joint integrity, and confidence.

Once the athlete owns the movement, we add light load. A kettlebell, a medicine ball, or a sandbag is usually more than enough. The load should teach the movement, not distort it.

Only when the athlete shows competence, consistency, and maturity do we move to heavier or more complex lifts. Even then, the goal is not maximal strength. The goal is filling gaps and building a broad base.

Youth athletes need variety more than they need intensity. They should push, pull, hinge, squat, carry, crawl, jump, throw, and sprint. They should hang from bars, climb ropes, and roll on the ground. The body learns through exposure.

The Matrix also keeps coaches honest. If a young athlete can bench press but cannot hang from a bar, there is a gap. If they can squat heavy but cannot skip or crawl smoothly, there is a gap. The Matrix shows us what is missing.

Over time, as the athlete grows and matures, the Matrix naturally evolves. Bodyweight becomes light load. Light load becomes moderate load. Play becomes structured training. But the categories never change.

That is the beauty of the system. It grows with the athlete.

The youth version of the Movement Matrix is not about building champions at twelve. It is about building capable, confident, and durable young people who can succeed in any sport they choose later.

If you fill the Matrix early, the athlete will thank you for the rest of their life.

Youth Movement Matrix by Age

Ages 8–11: The Play and Pattern Years

Primary Goal:

Learn how to move. Build coordination, balance, and confidence.

At this stage, training should look like **organized play**. Variety matters more than load. Skill matters more than sets and reps.

Movement Matrix

Squat

- Bodyweight squats

- Goblet squats with light loads

- Squat and hold games

Hinge

- Hip bridges

- Light kettlebell or dumbbell deadlifts

- Jumping and landing drills

Push

- Pushups (hands elevated if needed)

- Medicine ball chest passes

- Crawling patterns

Pull

- Ring rows
- Rope pulls
- Assisted chin-ups
- Hanging from bars

Carry

- Farmer walks with light weights
- Bear hugs with medicine balls
- Object carries during games

Core / Ground

- Crawling
- Rolling
- Tumbling
- Basic gymnastics shapes

Gait

- Running
- Skipping
- Hopping
- Agility games
- Tag

Throw

- Medicine ball throws
- Light object tossing
- Target games

Key Coaching Idea:
If it looks like recess, you're probably doing it right.

Ages 12–14: The Skill and Strength Introduction Years

Primary Goal:

Maintain movement variety while gradually introducing real strength training.

This is where structure can begin, but it must be done carefully. Some athletes are still children. Others look like adults. Treat the athlete in front of you, not the birth certificate.

Movement Matrix

Squat

- Goblet squats
- Front squat with light barbell
- Split squats

Hinge

- Kettlebell deadlifts
- Trap bar deadlifts (light to moderate)
- Jump variations

Push

- Pushups
- Dumbbell bench press
- Light barbell bench press
- Overhead press with light loads

Pull

- Chin-ups and pull-ups
- Inverted rows
- Band-assisted pulling

Carry

- Farmer walks
- Suitcase carries
- Front-loaded carries

Core / Ground

- Crawling
- Planks
- Basic rollouts
- Turkish get-up progressions

Gait

- Sprinting
- Change-of-direction drills
- Shuttle runs
- Sport-based movement

Throw

- Medicine ball throws (various directions)
- Rotational throws
- Overhead throws

Key Coaching Idea:
Teach technique. Do not chase numbers.

Ages 15–18: The Strength and Structure Years

Primary Goal:
Build real strength while maintaining athleticism and movement quality.

At this stage, most athletes can handle structured programs, but the coach must still respect individual development rates.

Movement Matrix

Squat

- Front squat

- Back squat

- Goblet squat (as accessory)

Hinge

- Trap bar deadlift

- Conventional or sumo deadlift

- Romanian deadlifts

- Explosive hinge work (jumps, swings)

Push

- Bench press

- Overhead press

- Dumbbell presses

- Pushups (various styles)

Pull

- Pull-ups and chin-ups

- Barbell or dumbbell rows

- Cable or band rows

Carry

- Heavy farmer walks

- Suitcase carries

- Front-loaded carries

- Offset carries

Core / Ground

- Planks and variations

- Rollouts

- Turkish get-ups
- Loaded carries as core work

Gait

- Sprinting
- Acceleration work
- Change-of-direction
- Conditioning runs

Throw

- Medicine ball power throws
- Rotational and overhead throws
- Sport-specific throwing practice

Key Coaching Idea:
Now we can load the patterns, but the patterns still come first.

Big Picture Summary

Across all three age groups:

The **movement categories never change**.

The **tools and loads change**.

The intent evolves from play → skill → strength.

8–11: Learn to move.
12–14: Learn to lift correctly.
15–18: Train for real strength and performance.

If a coach respects those three stages, most problems in youth training simply disappear

A Parent's Guide to Youth Strength Training

When parents ask me about training for their kids, they usually want to know one thing:

> *"What should my child be doing right now?"*

The answer depends less on the sport and more on the **stage of development**. A ten-year-old, a thirteen-year-old, and a seventeen-year-old may all be on the same team, but they are not in the same phase of life. Their training should reflect that.

What follows is a simple guide to help you understand what matters most at each stage.

Ages 8–11: Learn to Move

At this age, your child does not need a complicated program. They need to move, play, and explore.

The best things an 8–11-year-old can do include:

- Running
- Jumping
- Climbing
- Crawling
- Throwing
- Rolling
- Playing a variety of sports

Strength training, if introduced, should be simple and light:

- Bodyweight squats

- Pushups

- Light carries

- Hanging from bars

- Basic tumbling or gymnastics

What matters most:
Fun, variety, and confidence in movement.

If your child is smiling, sweating, and sleeping well at night, you are probably doing it right.

Ages 12–14: Learn the Skills of Strength

This is a transition phase. Some kids are still very much children. Others look like young adults. The key is not to rush.

At this age, athletes can begin learning real strength training, but the focus should be on:

- Good technique

- Light to moderate loads

- Simple, repeatable exercises

Good choices include:

- Goblet squats

- Trap bar deadlifts

- Pushups and presses

- Chin-ups or rows

- Farmer walks

- Medicine ball throws

They should still:

- Play multiple sports
- Run and jump often
- Avoid year-round specialization

What matters most:
Learning how to lift correctly, not how much they can lift.

Ages 15–18: Build Real Strength

By this stage, most athletes are ready for structured training. This is when the weight room can make a real difference.

Now we can:
- Squat with a barbell
- Deadlift
- Bench press
- Overhead press
- Do heavier carries
- Follow structured programs

But the principles still matter:
- Technique before load
- Strength before specialization
- Long-term health over short-term success

Athletes at this age should still:
- Move well
- Sprint
- Jump
- Play more than one sport when possible

What matters most:
Consistent, well-coached strength training built on good movement.

The Three Big Rules for Parents

If you remember nothing else, remember these three points.

1. Movement First

Before your child becomes a great athlete, they must become a good mover.

Running, jumping, crawling, climbing, and carrying build the foundation for everything else.

2. Avoid Early Specialization

Kids who play multiple sports tend to:

- Stay healthier
- Burn out less
- Become better overall athletes

One sport, year-round, at a young age often leads to overuse injuries and mental fatigue.

3. Strength Training Is Safe When Done Correctly

Properly coached strength training:

- Reduces injury risk
- Improves confidence
- Builds resilience

- Supports long-term athletic development

The key is **good coaching and appropriate loads**, not chasing records.

A Simple Test for Parents

Ask yourself three questions:

1. Is my child having fun?
2. Is my child moving in lots of different ways?
3. Is the training appropriate for their age and maturity?

If the answer to all three is yes, you are on the right path.

If the program looks like something designed for a professional athlete, it probably isn't right for your child.

Final Thought

The goal of youth sports is not to create a ten-year-old champion. The goal is to create a **healthy, capable, confident adult**.

If we keep that goal in mind, most of the right decisions become obvious.

Food, Supplements, and the Youth Athlete

Let me make this simple.

If you are coaching youth athletes and you are spending more time talking about supplements than sleep, you are doing it wrong.

If you are debating protein timing with a fourteen-year-old who lives on energy drinks and four hours of sleep, you are doing it wrong.

And if you think a powder will fix what parenting, cooking, and common sense have ignored, you are really doing it wrong.

First: They Are Growing Humans

A youth athlete is not a small professional athlete.

They are a growing human being.

Bones are lengthening. Hormones are fluctuating. Coordination is changing weekly. Sometimes daily. The appetite of a teenage boy can look like a competitive eating contest. The appetite of a teenage girl can disappear under stress and social pressure.

Your job is not to optimize macronutrient ratios. Your job is to support growth.

Growth requires:

- Enough total calories

- Protein from real food

- Fruits and vegetables

- Carbohydrates for activity

- Healthy fats

- Water

- Sleep

Notice what is not on that list: creatine stacks, fat burners, pre-workout cocktails, and anything sold in a black tub with lightning bolts on the label.

The First Nutrition Question

Before I ever talk about supplements with a young athlete, I ask one question:

Are you eating breakfast?

If the answer is no, we are done talking about supplements.

A simple breakfast of eggs, yogurt, fruit, oatmeal, or even a peanut butter sandwich solves more problems than most powders ever will.

The next question:

Are you drinking water?

Not sports drinks all day. Not energy drinks. Water.

Hydration fixes headaches, improves focus, and supports training. It is boring. It is also powerful.

Protein: Calm Down

Yes, athletes need protein. No, they do not need 300 grams a day.

A simple guideline works:

Have a source of protein at every meal.

That could be:

- Eggs
- Milk
- Greek yogurt
- Chicken
- Beef
- Beans
- Fish

If a young athlete eats three or four balanced meals a day with protein included, they are fine.

Most teenagers do not need a protein powder. They need a sandwich, a piece of fruit, and a glass of water.

Supplements: The Hard Truth

Here is what I tell parents.

If your child:

- Is sleeping eight to ten hours a night
- Is eating real meals
- Is drinking water
- Is training appropriately
- Is managing school stress

Then and only then can we even discuss supplementation.

And even then, the list is short.

A basic multivitamin? Fine.

Creatine for an older, post-puberty athlete under supervision? Possibly.

Vitamin D in northern climates? Often reasonable.

But most of what is marketed to youth athletes is unnecessary at best and harmful at worst.

The supplement industry thrives on insecurity.

"Your child will fall behind."

"No one else is working this hard."

"Unlock your genetic potential."

Nonsense.

The biggest performance enhancers for youth athletes are:

- Puberty
- Consistent training
- Sleep
- Food

In that order.

The Energy Drink Disaster

I once had an athlete misunderstand everything I said during a game. I finally pulled him to the sideline to ask what was wrong. He laid on the ground and asked for a milkshake. I immediately started on the concussion protocol.

I was wrong. He had overdosed on energy drinks before the game and was now in a medical situation. In case you are worried: everything turned out okay and I learned a big lesson.

If I could eliminate one thing from youth sports tomorrow, it would not be sugar. It would be energy drinks. The combination of caffeine, chronic stress, and adolescence is a volatile mix. Many young athletes are already navigating academic pressure, social dynamics, lack of sleep, and hormonal changes. Adding heavy stimulants to that environment rarely improves performance and often amplifies instability.

You cannot out-supplement poor sleep. You cannot stimulate your way into long-term development. A wired athlete is not necessarily a prepared athlete. Elevated heart rates, jittery focus, and artificial intensity may look productive in the short term, but they do not build sustainable strength or resilience.

> **If you want better performance, start with the simplest intervention available: teach them to go to bed.**

Body Image and the Weight Room

This is where coaching truly matters. The weight room can either become a place of growth or a place of distortion, depending on the guidance surrounding it. Young men often want to get big as quickly as possible. Young women are often pressured to get smaller. Both impulses can lead down unhealthy paths.

Crash dieting, extreme bulking, aggressive cutting phases, and constant comparison on social media can twist training into something it was never meant to be. Instead of building strength and confidence, it becomes about chasing an image. When appearance replaces performance as the primary goal, the training environment shifts in a dangerous direction.

Strength training for youth athletes should build confidence, competence, and resilience. It should help them feel capable in their bodies, not critical of them. The goal is durability and self-trust, not obsession.

Food plays a central role in this conversation. It is fuel, but it is also culture, family, celebration, and health. When we reduce it to a spreadsheet too early, we risk creating anxiety around something that should support growth. Teaching young athletes to eat balanced meals, recover properly, and respect hunger is far more valuable than handing them rigid numbers before they are ready to understand the context.

Handled correctly, the weight room becomes a place where young athletes learn what their bodies can do. Handled poorly, it becomes a place where they learn to judge what their bodies look like. Coaching makes the difference.

What Actually Works

For most youth athletes, nutrition success looks like this:

- Three meals a day
- One or two snacks
- Protein at each meal
- Fruits and vegetables daily
- Plenty of water
- Minimal ultra-processed junk
- Regular family meals when possible

That is not sexy. It works.

Add consistent strength training and multi-sport participation and you have done 95 percent of what matters.

Coaching the Parents on Nutrition

When I coach youth athletes, I am often really coaching the parents.

Parents need reassurance that:

- Their child does not need every new product.

- Normal growth includes awkward phases.

- Strength comes from years, not weeks.

If you are running a youth program, consider hosting a parent meeting. Explain the basics. Remove the mystery. Calm the noise.

Once parents understand that development is long-term, most of the supplement panic disappears.

The Long Game

The goal of youth training is not to create a shredded sixteen-year-old.

The goal is to create a healthy, strong, confident twenty-five-year-old.

If we build habits around real food, reasonable portions, good sleep, and consistent training, we win.

If we chase powders, shortcuts, and social media physiques, we lose.

It really is that simple.

Food Rules for Youth Athletes

(Simple. Boring. Effective.)

Rule 1: Eat Real Food

If your great-grandmother wouldn't recognize it as food, think twice.

Meat. Eggs. Milk. Yogurt. Rice. Potatoes. Fruit. Vegetables. Beans. Bread. Oats.

You do not need a chemistry degree to feed a young athlete.

Rule 2: Eat Breakfast

No athlete skips breakfast and thrives long term.

It does not need to be perfect. It needs to exist.

- Eggs and toast
- Yogurt and fruit
- Oatmeal and milk
- A sandwich and a banana

Breakfast beats supplements. Every time.

Rule 3: Protein at Every Meal

You do not need extreme protein intake. You need consistency.

Every meal should include a protein source:

- Eggs
- Chicken
- Beef
- Fish
- Milk
- Greek yogurt
- Beans

No math required. Just make sure it is there.

Rule 4: Drink Water

Water first.

Not energy drinks.
Not soda.
Not *"performance"* drinks all day long.

Hydration improves performance more reliably than most supplements ever will.

If urine is pale, you are probably doing fine.

Rule 5: Fruits and Vegetables Daily

You do not need exotic superfoods.

Just eat them.

- Apples
- Bananas
- Berries
- Carrots
- Broccoli
- Spinach
- Peppers

Color on the plate is usually a good sign.

Rule 6: Sleep Is a Nutrition Strategy

Eight to ten hours for most youth athletes.

If you are tired, no supplement fixes that.

Sleep drives recovery, growth, hormone balance, and learning. It is the most powerful *"performance enhancer"* available.

Rule 7: Snacks Are Fine

Young athletes burn fuel.

Snacks are not the enemy.

Good snack examples:

- Yogurt
- Fruit
- Nuts
- Sandwich
- Cheese and crackers
- Leftovers

A snack should look like food, not a science experiment.

Rule 8: Supplements Are the Last 1 Percent

Only consider supplements when:

- Meals are consistent
- Sleep is solid
- Hydration is good
- Training is appropriate

Even then, keep it simple:

- Basic multivitamin
- Vitamin D if needed
- Possibly creatine for older, post-puberty athletes under supervision

If someone promises dramatic results from a powder, be skeptical.

Rule 9: No Energy Drinks

Caffeine plus adolescence plus stress is not a performance plan.

If you need an energy drink to train, you need sleep.

Rule 10: Play the Long Game

The goal is not to look impressive at sixteen.

The goal is to be healthy, strong, and capable at twenty-five, forty, and sixty.

Food habits built now last a lifetime.

The Simple Checklist

Before worrying about macros, ask:

- Did you eat three real meals today?
- Did you drink water?
- Did you get protein at each meal?
- Did you eat at least one fruit and one vegetable?
- Did you sleep enough?

If the answer is yes, you are ahead of most of the field.

Simple.
Repeatable.
Sustainable.

And that wins in the long run.

Managing Compromises in Youth Sport Training

| *"Yes, we can."*

We have the resources. We went to the class. We read the book. With just a little information, we're eager to add something new and shiny to the system. And that, really, is the problem.

In youth sport training, everything probably works. I've built much of my career on the idea that ***"everything works."*** But this area is tricky: everything only *probably* works, and figuring out exactly what went right or wrong is mostly guesswork. The sheer volume of qualities needed to compete makes it hard to know whether a new idea, supplement, or program is actually helping.

And yet, your competition might be doing it. That forces you to ask tough questions:

- If they're adding this, do we need to add it too?

- Or are we in a different situation, with a different vision, meaning we don't need it at all?

- Or maybe, often enough, this new idea is simply idiotic, and ignoring it saves time and energy.

The Illusion of Progress

Visit a Division One or professional team facility and you'll see everything: machines, kettlebells, med balls, ropes, ski trainers. One college even bought a $25,000 machine purely for recruiting optics, and they never used it. Why? Because everyone else was doing it.

Programs pile on Strongman gear and Olympic bars, only to abandon them weeks later. Does it work? Who knows? Three months later there's a new toy.

That's the nature of youth sport training. It demands a special kind of thinking: managing compromises.

You can do anything, and it might work. But if you spend too much time chasing the next shiny idea, how do you keep doing what got you there in the first place? That's the tension.

A Lesson From Football

Many of my examples come from American football. It's a clear model for team strength training and also for some of its worst excesses. If you don't follow football, that's fine. The broader lessons apply.

At every Super Bowl party, some fan says, ***"Team X just needs to run this play."*** It's laughable. NFL teams already run everything. More importantly, they can't switch from one system to another overnight.

Years ago, Urban Meyer's staff at University of Utah shook up college football with the Spread Offense. Players were sent all over the field, mixing pass-heavy attacks with option runs. But other systems, like the Veer, still thrived.

Bob Ladouceur at De La Salle High School explained why the Veer works:

> ***"Nothing is more demoralizing to a team than having an offense move the ball down the field by running and controlling the football."***

The upside: your offensive line becomes your defense. The downside: if you fall behind, it's tough to score quickly.

Contrast that with a dad in the stands yelling, ***"Throw the ball more!"***

If you run a pass-heavy system, your linemen step back three steps on every snap. In the Veer, they drive forward three. Try to do both at once and you stand still.

The Key: Managing Compromises

So yes, you can do anything in youth sport training, and it might help. But the real key to success is managing compromises.

In these sports, people constantly say, ***"We've got to get back to..."*** and fill in the blank. Drift from one idea to the next and soon you've forgotten the basics that led to success.

> ***The old football coach phrase sums it up:***
> ***"You dance with the girl who brung ya."***

But how do you stay faithful to the basics while exploring new ideas, especially when your competition seems to be mastering them?

You manage compromises.

Be careful. The word *decide* comes from a root meaning to cut or kill. Make too sharp a turn and you may throw the baby out with the bathwater. Suddenly, like the lineman who's been driving forward all season and is now told to step back, you're at a standstill.

Can Being Decisive Backfire?

Absolutely.

I once coached on a staff that adopted the Run and Shoot offense. It confused defenses, created big plays, and by late in the half we often scored easily. I even thought a hidden benefit was conditioning. Our games lasted longer, and we were prepared for that. The opponents weren't.

But what really worked was keeping our old I-formation, ***"punch you in the mouth"*** plays. At halftime, opposing coaches redrew their defenses to stop the Run and Shoot. Then we'd come out and run Blasts and Powers, scoring quickly.

The next season we decided to simplify. Just run the Run and Shoot. It was easier to teach, install, and run.

We also started losing. A lot.

It was easier for defenses to prepare for one face of our offense.

That's managing compromises. You can get too cute or too simple. Either way, you risk your success.

So How Do You Manage Compromises?

1. Build absolute strength across the roster.
A team with solid strength levels from top to bottom beats one with superstars and weak links. That's why I created the Big Blue Club for boys and the Big Silver Club for girls.

2. Align strength and conditioning with your program's vision.
If the head coach wants a fast, high-speed game, your offseason looks like track practice. If it's smash-mouth football, your offseason is prowlers and sleds.

3. Rigorously evaluate and assess.
I'm a big believer in the philosophy of Bill Walsh: winning is a byproduct of standards of excellence. John Wooden taught the same lesson. Success comes from a clear vision of what matters, executed consistently.

Excellence in the Details
Youth sport programs demand excellence in everything. You can't have filthy locker rooms and sloppy equipment and still call yourself first class. Whether it's the weight room or the toilet facilities, it all matters.

Leading people is also about managing compromises. Everyone wants Christmas week off, so as the boss, you figure it out. Parenting is managing compromises every day.

"Why does Billy get a bigger bowl?"
"It's the same amount."
"But his bowl is bigger."

"Here, take a bigger bowl."

It never ends.

The art is keeping your eyes on the mission while sorting through new ways to achieve it, never forgetting the two core mantras of life:

The mission is to keep the mission the mission.
The goal is to keep the goal the goal.

Summary: Managing Compromises in Sport Training

Challenge	Response
Everything seems viable	Test prudently; avoid novelty for its own sake
Pressure to imitate peers	Ask: does this serve our mission?
New ideas vs fundamentals	Keep the core first; integrate selectively
Strategy drift	Dance with the one who brung you
Leadership decisions	Accept trade-offs; stay mission-focused

Level Changes: The Missing Ingredient in Youth Strength Training

The biggest gaps in training show up in real life.

You see it when someone hikes.
You see it when someone helps a friend move.
You see it when someone has to get down on the floor and get back up.

Two weaknesses appear over and over:

Authentic squatting.
Loaded carries.

Not accordion squatting.
Not machines.
Not seated leg presses.

Real squats.
Real carries.

Add goblet squats and farmer walks to almost anyone's program and things improve quickly.

Do them.

But there is another gap. More subtle. More important.

A lack of levels.

What Are Levels?

When I say *"levels,"* I mean where your body is in relation to the ground.

On your back.
Prone.
Six-point. (Hands, knees, and feet on the ground)
Bear. (Hands and feet on the ground, knees raised)
Half-kneeling.
Standing tall.
Moving through space.

Most machine training programs live in one level.

Seated.
Strapped in.
Select the load.
Move the handle.

That doesn't reflect life. It doesn't reflect sport. It doesn't reflect youth.

Kids live on the floor.

They roll.
They crawl.
They kneel.
They pop up.
They sprint away.

Then we sit them in machines and wonder what's missing.

The Floor Is the Secret

The fitness industry thrives on secrets.

Fat-burning secrets.
Six-pack ab secrets.
Speed secrets.

Here's mine:

The floor.

It's free. It's always available. And most people avoid it.

In assessments, I ask people to get down and back up off the floor. Some look at it like it's a cliff.

"All the way down there?"

Yes. All the way down there.

If a young athlete cannot comfortably get down and up, we've skipped steps.

Earth. Human. Sky.

Years ago, I learned three movement categories from a dance instructor influenced by Martha Graham:

Earth.
Human.
Sky.

She meant it artistically. I heard it developmentally. And once I filtered youth training through that lens, things made more sense.

Earth
On your back.
Prone.
Six-point.
Bear.
Half-kneeling.

Human
Air.
Hang.
Brachiate.

Sky
Squat.
Hinge.
Gait.

Carry.

Youth training should touch all three.

If a program never leaves Sky, it's incomplete.
If it never returns to Earth, it's fragile.

Development Follows Levels

Youth development already follows this pattern:

Roll.
Crawl.
Kneel.
Stand.
Run.
Fall.
Get back up.

That's life.

It's also a training template. When we remove levels, we remove development.

When we keep athletes upright and loaded all the time, we rob them of coordination and resilience. Level changes do something powerful:

They elevate heart rate.
They challenge orientation.
They demand awareness.
They build work capacity.

And they look like life.

Lift-N-Sprints

We've used lift-n-sprints for decades.

Pick a hinge or squat variation.
Do eight to ten reps.

Drop the load.
Sprint immediately.

No delay.

Three rounds is enough.

If you feel like you could do more, increase quality next time.

For youth athletes this teaches:

Level change.
Force production.
Transition under fatigue.
Athletic aggression.

It's not conditioning: It's integration.

Small Space Solutions

Not everyone has room to sprint.

Try this:

Eight goblet squats
Prowler push 20–40 meters
Eight push-ups

Up to five rounds.

You'll feel the cost of getting up and down.

Other simple options:

Swings
Goblet squats
Push-ups (This combo is the Humane Burpee)

Deadlifts
Bear crawls (This easy to teach combination *"feels"* like the game a professional football player told me)

The exercise list matters less than the level change.

Testing That Reflects Life

For one football team, we used:

Five deadlifts with the Trap Bar (at least bodyweight)
Bear crawl 10 yards
Sprint 20 yards (all for time)

That tells you more about readiness than a seated machine circuit ever will.

For javelin throwers, we warmed up with this amazing combination:

Goblet squats
Monkey bars
Bear crawl (all in a quick circuit)

It built mobility, strength, breathing — and fun.

That last word matters. Youth training should be demanding. It should also be enjoyable.

From Earth to Sky: The Developmental Ladder

There's a tendency in youth strength training to start where things look impressive.

Barbells.
Vertical loading.
Heavy carries.
Squats that look good on video.

That's Sky.

And Sky matters. But development doesn't start there.

Children begin on Earth.

They roll before they crawl.
They crawl before they stand.

They stand before they run.

No one rushes that sequence-except in training!

Earth work isn't remedial. It's neurological.

Rolling, crawling, bridging, half-kneeling, ground-based pushes and pulls build:

Cross-body coordination.
Reflexive core stability.
Shoulder integrity.
Hip awareness.

Skip Earth and you skip wiring.

The Human level comes next.

Jumping.
Skipping.
Bounding.
Hanging.
Climbing.

This is elasticity. Rhythm. Timing. Modern youth programs often underdose it.

Kids don't hang enough.
They don't climb enough.
They don't move dynamically enough without load.

If Earth builds control, Human builds expression.

Sky builds force. Sky is squats, hinges, carries, presses, pulls, loaded gait. But Sky should be earned. Before aggressive loading, a young athlete should demonstrate:

Ground control.
Dynamic expression.
Positional ownership.

If they cannot control half-kneeling, crawl contralaterally, hang, or land quietly, adding load is not progression.

It's impatience.

How This Fits the Youth Model

This ladder reinforces everything we've discussed:

Development before display.
Movement quality before load.
Exposure before specialization.
Breadth before narrowing.

A youth athlete who only trains in Sky becomes narrow early. One who moves across Earth, Human, and Sky becomes adaptable.

And adaptability wins long-term.

Age Integration

Ages 6–10
Earth dominates.
Human is constant.
Sky is light and technical.

Ages 11–14
Earth remains.
Human expands.
Sky load increases gradually.

Ages 15+
Sky becomes more prominent.
Earth and Human remain for restoration and resilience.

Earth never disappears.
Human never disappears.

If they do, development stalls.

The Fractal of a Training Day

A fractal is a repeating pattern in nature: a leaf resembles a tree and a small rock can look like a mountai.

A training day should resemble a career.

Start on the ground.
Rise up.
Move hard.
Stumble.
Get back up.
Finish better than you started.

If a session reflects the arc of development, we're on the right track.

The Real Goal

The goal isn't fatigue. It isn't novelty. It isn't complexity.

It's development. If a young athlete can:

Roll smoothly.
Crawl confidently.
Kneel comfortably.
Squat authentically.
Hinge powerfully.
Carry with posture.
Sprint with intent.

We're building something durable.

If they can only sit and push a machine, we're not.

The Long Game

Youth strength training isn't about how much a 13-year-old can squat.

It's about what their shoulders feel like at 23.
Whether their hips still move at 30.
Whether they still enjoy training at 40.

Humans develop from the ground up.

Earth builds the foundation.

Human builds the bridge.
Sky builds the structure.

Foundations and bridges still matter long after the structure stands.

If we respect the ladder, we protect the athlete.

And youth training should always protect the athlete.

Chapter Fifteen

Standards

I've been asked about standards since the first day I started to coach. And, and, and...I have been trying to explain from that first day that standards in the weightroom are simply that:

These are the things we EXPECT you to be able to do at this level of play. For NCAA Division One football, the number I hear most often is 3-4-5:

300 pound clean (135kg)

400 pound bench press (180kg)

500 pound back squat (225 kg)

Doctor Tom Fahey taught us almost a generation ago that an elite male discus thrower should be able to do the following:

400 bench press (180kg)

250 snatch`(115kg)

300 clean (135kg)

450 back squat (205kg)

Looking at those numbers from the prism of a professional football team or a group of elite throwers, the first response is:

Aren't these a little low?

And that's the catch with standards. I've taught at academically elite schools and the students are simply expected to show up on-time, prepared for class, and in full uniform.

That's the STANDARD. In geometry, these are the *"givens."* If one is asked to be in a wedding party, the standard is probably formal wear. A filthy t-shirt and flip-flops just won't usually cut it.

So, basically, standards are not the minimum, not the maximum, but simply what we expect as a program.

A few notes before I share my high school varsity standards. First, there are many, many athletes who will not be able to qualify for these clubs and still excel at the high school level. I do think these levels are reachable by a large proportion of the teenage athletic pool if the work is done.

"If the work is done" forecasts a lot of issues later on in life!

There is a large learning curve on many of these lifts. Foundational work must be put in and there needs to be repetitions.

> *"Foundational work must be put in and there needs to be repetitions." This might seem like a cliché-fest but the experienced coach will find truth here.*

Finally, the following two clubs come from decades of experience and work with literally thousands of athletes. On the girls' side, these represent at least a thousand student-athletes training hard. I first started training female athletes and interested women in the late 1970s and there was very little information on training women available early in my career. I really appreciate the insights of the pioneers of women's lifting including my two friends, Jan Todd and Carol Cady, who shared so much history and knowledge with me. So, here you go:

Big Blue Club (Boys)
- Power Clean 205 pounds (95 kilos)
- Deadlift 315 pounds (145 kilos)

- Back Squat 255 pounds (120 kilos)
- Front Squat 205 pounds (95 kilos)
- Standing Press 115 pounds (55 kilos)
- One Arm Bench 32 kilos x 5 right /5 left
- Power Clean and Jerk 165 pounds (75 kilos)

Big Silver Club (Girls)

- Power Clean 95 pounds (45 kilos)
- Deadlift 205 pounds (95 kilos)
- Back Squat 135 pounds (65 kilos)
- Front Squat 95 pounds (45 kilos)
- Standing Press 70 pounds (35 kilos)
- One Arm Bench 12 kilos x 10 right /10 left
- Power Clean and Jerk 75 pounds (35 kilos)

The first goal was to make all these lifts. Then, to join the club, all the lifts had to be done in one lifting session. Generally, an athlete had one lagging lift to attain the full list and when that was mastered making the club was easy.

My advanced athletes, boys and girls at around age 17, once staged a mini-contest to see who could do all seven challenges the fastest. I didn't think it was a good idea, except it was my daughter's idea... so, here we go!

Oh, and somebody ALWAYS asks about the standard for the bench press. I have always taught that the power clean, front squat, and bench press should always be *"around"* the same. So, boys should bench 205 and girls 95.

Before I close this discussion on standards, I do want to remind everyone that it takes time to reach these standards. As a team, it is much more valuable to have the entire team reach these standards rather than one or two. I once sent the varsity football coach 62 young men who were all in the Big Blue Club.

We did very, very well that season. Our scout team and back up players were as physically dominate as most team's starters.

This is example sums the role of the youth strength coach: it is building up the entire team that allows success. Don't just focus on the stars. Reminder: today's stars might be left in the dust by the hard-working substitutes striving to be better in every way.

It's often the truth.

A Middle School/ Junior High Program

(I've written about my junior high program since I first did it well over fifty years ago. At Southwood, our physical education program taught us marching, wrestling, lifting, sports and games, and countless tests...including written exams. I'm still influenced by the simplicity and soundness. Starting each day with a uniform check, 800 meters of running followed by an obstacle course, calisthenics, and basic stretching and THEN the class helped me realize my athletic and academic dreams. I hope you too can use this material.)

I graduated from Catholic elementary school in 1971. After eight years at St. Veronica's, I transferred to Southwood Junior High to begin a new journey. It was an interesting transition. Moving from Irish nuns to public school was big enough, but I was also going to play football. At 118 pounds of pure *"too small,"* it was obvious to everyone that I needed to lift weights.

It was at this time that I was introduced to Southwood's lifting program. In a portable building, the school had laid out about fifteen of those cement-filled weightlifting sets that everyone from my generation remembers as their first barbell.

Mr. Dave Freeman spent little time explaining the *"rep–set"* system of 8–6–4 because everybody, except me, already knew what to do. That was part of the brilliance of the program. You learned it once, then you lifted. It was a program that stayed with me for my entire career.

The structure was simple. Groups of four boys were given a bar. The bars ranged from very light, maybe twenty-five pounds, up to nearly a hundred pounds. Each boy lifted, put the bar down, and the next boy went. The four rotated from lifter to watcher, and the bar never stopped moving. The three sets did not take long. In fact, sometimes it was hard to catch your breath before your next turn.

The reps were simple:

- First set: 8 repetitions

- Second set: 6 repetitions

- Third set: 4 repetitions

The goal was clear. When you completed all eighteen reps, you moved to the next barbell at the next session. Some students progressed slowly, but others soon found themselves using the heaviest bar.

Like me!

The program involved four lifts:

- Power clean

- Military press

- Front squat

- Bench press

Each lift followed the 8–6–4 format. The bar was cleaned once for the set of military presses and once for the front squats. So, in each workout, the athlete cleaned the bar from the ground to the chest twenty-two times. If, as some people say, the power clean is the king of the exercises, that is a lot of time spent with the king.

To speed things up, there were times when Mr. Freeman recommended combining the power clean and military press. One clean followed by one press, repeated for eight reps with a lighter weight. You could then move right into the front squats. This combination of power clean, military press, and front squat remains the foundation of my armor building workouts all these years later.

Each day began with a warm-up of two laps and an obstacle course. The laps were about six hundred meters. The obstacle course included a wall, various upper-body challenges, and some balance work. All in all, it was a solid program.

Three days a week, the workout looked like this:

- Power clean: 8–6–4

- Military press: 8–6–4

- Front squat: 8–6–4

- Bench press: 8–6–4

Mr. Freeman also kept the weight room open before and after school. Throughout my career, I have done the same. Some of my best training insights came from those extra sessions with students and other faculty members.

He and the rest of the PE staff also did something that still makes me think, ***"This is genius."*** Three times a year, we were tested over three days in ten or twelve events. We trained for these tests for weeks. I can remember most of them:

- Pull-ups

- Push-ups

- Sit-ups

- Shuttle run

- 40-yard dash

- 600-yard run

- Six-minute run

Each event was scored, and we accumulated points. Some of my classmates had it all figured out. I was told that adding one pull-up was worth more points than improving the 600-yard run by a certain margin, and it was easier. We worked on our weak events during free periods and asked each other for advice.

The day after testing, Mr. Freeman handed out the awards: various colored felt triangles. As I recall, white was the entry level. From there, it moved to blue, red, green, black, and finally gold. Guys trained for months trying to earn the gold triangle.

Read that again: a gold felt triangle. It was a piece of cheap gold-colored felt cut into a triangle to be sewn or, in my case, glued onto our PE shorts.

You might miss the point. Thirteen- and fourteen-year-old boys took time away from adolescent nonsense to train hard and smart just to earn a piece of felt. This was my first introduction to the power of standards and measurements. If you want someone to achieve, put up a barrier and tell them to jump over it. Then raise the barrier.

My brother Gary, who has a rare gift for making people angry, often notes that the problem with modern education is that they set the high jump bar at one foot. All the kids clear the bar and receive a gold medal. The kids know it is a joke and throw the medals away later.

In 1971 and 1972, Coach Freeman simply offered different colors of felt. Some of my classmates did not care at all, and many of them did not amount to much athletically. But to the rest of us, that piece of felt was worth sweating for in our free time.

Mr. Freeman also coached football, basketball, and track. He was always fair and answered every question I ever had. He was a coach's coach.

As I remember him, I realize how much I have modeled myself after him.

There are three basic ways to use the Southwood workout.

The first is the classic approach: one bar and one weight for all four exercises. What limits the athlete here is the military press. The upside is that athletes are not afraid to go deep in the front squat with the lighter weight. Since I believe depth is more important than load in the early learning process, this variation may be the best for beginners. Of course, the kids know they can bench much more, so they often do extra sets on their own after the formal workout. I never saw that as a real problem.

The second variation is to change the weight for each exercise. The front squat is still limited by the power clean, but early in the learning process, less weight on the front squat is usually fine. I am still a believer in movement over muscles, and correct movement over heavy weight. A six-hundred-pound front squat is not a *"quad exercise."* You need the whole body for that. And if you barely bend your knees, do not brag about your big squat.

In large groups, this variation requires a lot of plate changing. But for groups of twenty or fewer, or for individuals, it works very well.

The third variation is to use the Southwood workout as a warm-up. I know everyone believes they are advanced now, but there is something powerful about performing four big movements to prepare the body. Like Armor Building Formula complexes, there is also some fat loss built into this whole-body work.

For fun, try performing the eight power cleans, military presses, and front squats back to back. Then continue with the six-rep sets and finish with the fours. I experimented with adding the bench press to this cluster, but it required too much wrestling with the bar. It was simply too taxing for a warm-up, and safety became a concern.

From the Southwood program, we progress to the **Big Five** workout. This is a simple linear progression using five sets of five reps on the same four lifts, with deadlifts added.

The workout looks like this:
- Power clean: 5 × 5
- Military press: 5 × 5
- Front squat: 5 × 5
- Bench press: 5 × 5
- Deadlift (any variation): 5 × 5

This is a classic approach. The late Reg Park used it with great success, and one of his famous admirers followed a similar plan (that would be Arnold!).

I have my athletes add weight each set so that the fifth set is as heavy as they can manage. With young male and female athletes, it is not unusual for them to be within ten pounds of their max single for five reps. You do not see this in lifters with more experience, but with beginners it happens often.

Every fifth workout, we change the rep scheme. Instead of five sets of five, we do three sets: a set of five, add weight, a set of three, add weight, and then a heavy double. This is the 5–3–2 workout, and the goal is to go as heavy as possible on the double.

Heavy singles with young athletes often lead to what I call fuzzy logic. Spotters help *"a little,"* squat depth gets questionable, legs sneak into the presses, and so on. With a double, I can at least be sure that one of the reps was legitimate. We do not want fuzzy maxes in the weight room.

I moved to the every-fifth-session 5–3–2 workout because I noticed my athletes improving as the volume from the five-by-fives built up. An easier test day every couple of weeks kept enthusiasm high. I do not worry about boring athletes when they are making progress. There is nothing worse than a program that is both boring and non-progressive. Sadly, that describes many training programs.

After three or four weeks on the Southwood program, we shift to the Big Five. After about two months on the Big Five, with several opportunities to lift heavy, the athletes are ready to move on to other programs.

By then, there is a visible level of mastery in the five major lifts. There is also a lot more weight on the bars. I have seen sophomores power clean over two hundred pounds for a set of five. That is good lifting for an adult and remarkable for a fifteen-year-old.

The Southwood and Big Five programs are just two of the tools I use to introduce students to the world of lifting, fitness, and health. Many of them fully buy into the process. They clean up their diets, add a protein shake around training, and stay consistent. The gains in strength and muscle are impressive.

After a few weeks of battling the weights, my students are ready for anything.

Tumbling

(Do not worry about the specific names or how to perform each movement that follows. The goal is simple: introduce tumbling at every level.)

As a child, I took a local course in judo. Being the youngest of six, and one of five boys, I suddenly found myself very comfortable on the mats, tossing around people my own size. That was a first for me.

Judo had long term benefits that I still appreciate. Learning how to fall, how to be thrown, and how to get back up without injury has helped me on icy sidewalks, on slippery shower floors, and during sports.

I still have film of my final high school football game, and I can point to at least three plays where I used what I learned in judo to defeat the ball carrier and his blockers.

When I decided to advance my weightlifting, I picked up Myles Callum's **Body-Building and Self-Defense**. A surprising amount of space was devoted to tumbling. He recommended movements like forward and backward rolls, headstands, handstands, cartwheels, backbends, and flips. It was a great list, though I never mastered the flips outside of diving boards at the pool.

Tumbling was also part of my school physical education programs, but like rope climbing, it has largely disappeared from most curricula.

With the rise of mixed martial arts, tumbling returned in a different form. In *Inside the Lion's Den*, Ken Shamrock included many tumbling style drills under the term ***"scrambling"***: rope drills, belly rolls to bridges, kip ups, duck walks, cartwheels, and leapfrog drills.

Tumbling can be taught as a stand-alone section or blended into the training week. I used to have athletes tumble on Wednesdays, and later I added it into daily training. A typical Wednesday session included forward rolls, shoulder rolls, dive rolls, side rolls, backward rolls, leapfrogs, wheelbarrows, hand balances, and cartwheels. Again, the exact names are not important. The idea is to move.

I have always loved circuit training for large groups, so we built workouts that included tumbling. A simple circuit looked like this:

1. Front squats

2. Bench press

3. Hurdle walkovers

4. Tumbling run on mats: cartwheel left, cartwheel right, shoulder roll left, shoulder roll right

5. Power snatch
   Then back to front squats.

Once, an opposing team walked into the weight room while our sophomores were running this circuit. I heard one player say, ***"We don't have a chance."*** He was right.

Do your best to bring tumbling back into training. At my age, the most dangerous thing in the home is the floor. If a school or program cannot afford mats, you can still teach a simple variation I call Get Back Ups.

Get Back Ups (GBUps)

Many people spend almost no time on the ground. So, I created a simple drill that doubles as conditioning, mobility, and movement education.

I call it Get Back Ups.

A crucial coaching tip

Do not overcoach this.
In fact, intentionally undercoach it.

Basic method

- With everyone standing, call out a position on the floor. Examples: on your front, on your left side, on your right side, on your back, or pushup position.

1. Wait until everyone settles.

2. Say: ***"Get back up."***

3. Once everyone is standing still, call the next position.

4. Add speed as appropriate!

That's it.

Different series restrict hand placement: hands free, one hand on a knee, opposite hand to knee, hands in pockets, hands behind the head, and so on. Each series uses the same sequence of positions.

After five series, the group has done twenty-five up and down reps. By the end, everyone is warm, sweating, and moving better.

Why it works

- People discover new strategies as movement is restricted.

- Older clients simplify their patterns and learn to use their legs and hips.

- It improves performance on tests like the sitting rising test.

- Most importantly, it builds the skill of getting up off the floor.

A Larger Point

Tumbling and groundwork serve a bigger purpose than just athletic development.

I grew up in a home where the realities of war were personal. When my brothers were fighting in Vietnam, my mother cried every day. My father had experienced the horrors of the Second World War firsthand. Military service was not an abstraction in our house.

Because of that, I get frustrated when the fitness industry sells the image of ***"training like special operations"*** or uses camouflage as a fashion statement. Real service is not a marketing theme.

From my family and friends in the military, I learned two important lessons.

Lesson One: Situational awareness

Many young people today lack awareness of their surroundings. I see groups of teens in airports, staring at their devices, blocking walkways, unaware of anyone around them.

In a college criminology class, we were taught a simple rule: listen to your inner voice. If a place feels wrong, it probably is. If a person gives off bad vibes, pay attention.

Warfare is situational awareness at the highest level, with threats from every direction. I am not asking for that level of vigilance. I am simply asking people to look up, assess their surroundings, and move with awareness.

Tumbling helps build this awareness. Moving on the ground, rolling, and navigating around others teaches awareness of hands, feet, and bodies. Parkour, obstacle courses, crawling, climbing, and varied environments all build the same skill.

A treadmill asks very little of your ankles or attention. A mountain trail demands awareness and teaches your body how to adjust, twist, and recover.

Lesson Two: Survive the first ten seconds

I grew up with a father, uncles, aunts, cousins, and brothers who fought and were wounded in America's wars. My mother kept us together throughout the insanity of having someone off to war. We didn't always talk about the realities of fighting, but when we did...we did. Around our dinner table, I learned a simple truth: if you survive the first ten seconds of a firefight, you will probably survive the battle. After the initial clash, it becomes a long, grinding effort.

Training should reflect this.

The body thrives on:
- Very short, high intensity efforts.

- Very long, steady movement.

The alactic system, short bursts of power, is often overlooked. Rest pause training is a good example: one heavy rep, rest ten seconds, repeat. Olympic lifters and some powerlifters use similar methods.

High intensity work builds muscle, strength, and performance, but it requires skill and courage under heavy loads.

On the other side, soldiers still have to walk to the fight. Rucking, loaded carries, sled dragging, and long walks build work capacity and resilience. If you can carry your bodyweight for distance, many other tasks become easier.

Your high intensity work usually comes from the hinge family: cleans, snatches, swings, and deadlifts. Your loaded carries get you to the fight. This is how you thrive; this is how you survive.

Summary: The Role of Tumbling

- Tumbling teaches people how to fall and get up safely.

- It builds coordination, awareness, and confidence.

- It can be integrated into warm ups, circuits, or conditioning.

- Simple drills like Get Back Ups provide most of the benefits without special equipment.

- Ground work improves real world movement and resilience.

Conclusion: What Are the Best Things?

If you strip all of this down to the essentials, the best things you can add to training are simple and timeless:

1. **Tumble and move on the ground.**
   Learn to fall, roll, and get back up.

2. **Practice situational awareness.**
   Move in varied environments, not just on machines.

3. **Train the hinge.**
   Swings, cleans, snatches, and deadlifts build real power.

4. **Carry heavy things and walk.**

Farmer walks, rucking, and loaded carries build the engine.

5. **Mix short, intense efforts with long, easy movement.**
   Sprints and heavy lifts on one end. Long walks on the other.

In short:

> *Hinge. Carry. Walk. Tumble. Pay attention. Get back up. And get home.*

Those are the foundations that serve athletes, soldiers, and ordinary people for a lifetime.

On Youth Development

Youth training is not a race.

It is not a highlight reel.
It is not a scholarship strategy.
It is not a shortcut to relevance.

It is preparation for a lifetime in a body.

Children are not unfinished adults. They are developing organisms. Bones are lengthening. Hormones are shifting. Coordination comes and goes in waves. Confidence is fragile. Identity is forming.

If we impose adult performance standards too early, we distort the process.

The purpose of youth training is simple:

Build movement competency.
Build strength patiently.
Build confidence quietly.
Build habits that last decades.

The strongest sixteen-year-old in the room is not necessarily the most successful twenty-five-year-old.

Early dominance often means early specialization.
Early specialization often means early burnout.

Our job is not to win at thirteen.
Our job is to raise capable adults.

Appendix One: Control First. Load Later. Long Game Always.

Youth training fails when ego enters the room.

Ego from parents.
Ego from coaches.
Ego from the athlete.

The body does not care about your timeline.
It adapts to stress when it is ready — not when we demand it.

Everything below follows one rule:

Movement earns load.

I. Youth Strength Standards

(If They Can't Control It, They Don't Load It.)

Ages 6–8 — Learn the Body

Can they squat without collapsing?
Can they crawl?
Can they hang?
Can they hop and land without noise?

No barbells.
No max testing.
Just movement.

If it looks awkward, that's fine.
If it looks painful, regress.

Ages 9–11 — Own Bodyweight

Before adding weight, they should own:

15 clean squats

5–10 push-ups

1–3 chin-ups

A stable hinge

A controlled plank

If they can't control their own body, they are not ready to control a barbell.

Ages 12–14 — Build the Base

Now we can teach load.

Goblet squats.
Trap bar deadlifts around bodyweight.
Push-ups and chin-ups progressing steadily. If appropriate, introduce the Olympic and Power lifts.

No grinders.
No ego lifts.
No public comparisons.

Technique is the standard. Not numbers.

Ages 15–18 — Earn the Right to Be Strong

Relative strength matters now.

But even here:

A technically perfect 1.3× bodyweight squat beats an ugly double bodyweight disaster.

Strength without position is a liability.

II. Readiness to Load

(This Is the Filter.)

Before weight increases, ask:

Can they control the eccentric?

Can they pause at the bottom?

Do the knees stay stable?

Does the spine stay neutral?

If the answer is inconsistent, the load stays the same.

If reps turn into grinding, we went too far.

If pain appears, we went too far.

Progression is earned through repeatable excellence — not occasional hero reps.

III. Food Rules

(Fuel Growth. Don't Complicate It.)

Young athletes do not need optimization.

They need:

Three real meals

Protein at each meal

Fruits and vegetables daily

Water

Eight to ten hours of sleep

Most supplement conversations are distractions from basic discipline.

If a fourteen-year-old is asking about creatine but skipping breakfast, we have lost perspective.

Food is not a hack.
It is a foundation.

The Core Principle

Development follows order:

Coordination
Control
Movement literacy
Relative strength
Absolute strength

Skip the early steps and the ceiling lowers.

Respect the sequence and the ceiling rises.

That is the work.

Quiet. Consistent. Patient.

And powerful.

Appendix Two: To the 14-Year-Old Who Wants to Get Big Fast

(This is something I wish I would have known at 14. Basically, I am writing this to little Danny in 1971.)

I get it.

You want abs. You want sleeves that stretch. You want someone at school to say, *"Have you been lifting?"* You want to look in the mirror and see something impressive looking back at you. That's normal. That's not vanity, that's being fourteen.

But let me tell you something nobody tells you clearly: the things that make you look impressive at 14 are not the things that make you impressive at 25.

At 14, you think muscles are everything. At 25, people notice competence. They notice confidence. They notice whether you can walk into a room and carry yourself well. They notice whether you can perform when it matters. They notice whether you are strong, capable, and reliable — not just whether your shirt fits tight.

Here's the truth: chasing *"big fast"* almost always costs you something later. It costs you movement quality. It costs you athleticism. Sometimes it costs you your knees, your shoulders, or your love for training. When you rush growth, you build a body that looks ready before it actually is ready.

What makes you impressive at 25? Showing up consistently. Learning the basics. Mastering push, pull, hinge, squat, and carry. Getting strong slowly. Eating like an adult. Sleeping like it matters. Playing sports. Moving well. Building a body that works.

Strength built patiently stays. Muscles rushed into existence disappear just as quickly.

Right now, your job isn't to specialize. It isn't to bulk hard. It isn't to live in the mirror. Your job is to become durable. To become coordinated. To become coachable. To become the kind of athlete that older lifters respect because you move well and listen.

You don't need to look impressive yet. You need to become impressive.

Trust me on this: the young athlete who learns discipline, who practices the basics, who builds strength brick by brick...that athlete wakes up at 25 with something far more valuable than abs.

He wakes up capable.

And capable never goes out of style.

Appendix Three: Movement Matrix

Movement	Planks as a Program	Strength Training (Less then 10 reps) / Hypertrophy (15-25 reps)	Anti-Rotation Work	Traids	Olympic Lifts
Push	**PUPPs** Plank	(Bench) Press Push-up	1 Arm Bench Press 1 Arm Overhead Press	Push press / jerk Swing Liftsprints, Liftsleds	Squat Snatch Clean & Jerk
Pull	**TRX Rows** Bat Wing Ts and Ys	Pull-up Row	1 arm TRX Row		
Hinge	**Gluteal Bridge** with AB Hold	Hip Thrust Rack DLs Goat Bag Swing	**Hill Sprints / Stadium Steps** Skipping / Bounding / High Knee Work		
Squat	**Goblet Squats** 6 point Rocks	Dbl KB Front Squat The Whole Squat Family	**Bear Hug Carries** Bear Crawls Bear Hug Carries with Monster Walk		
Loaded Carry	**Farmer's Walk** Horn Walk	Prowler Car push	1 arm carries: **Suitcase Carry** Waiter Walk Rack Walk		

About Dan John

Dan John has spent more than sixty years lifting heavy things and trying to figure out why people make fitness so complicated. A former All-American discus thrower, Highland Games athlete, and Olympic lifter, Dan somehow turned throwing stuff and picking up iron into a career as a coach, teacher, and author.

He's written books like Intervention, Can You Go?, and Now What?, each one trying (again) to answer the age-old question: ***"Why aren't people doing the simple stuff that actually works?"*** Known for reducing tangled training ideas into plain English—usually with a story about coaching, parenting, or his own spectacular mistakes—Dan travels the world teaching workshops that mix humor, insight, and a healthy dose of common sense.

When he's not coaching or writing, you'll find him in Utah, gardening, lifting, reading, and trying to keep up with his grandkids—who've already outpaced his speed but haven't quite beaten his deadlift. Yet.

NEVER LET GO